KANYE WEST

MUSIC INDUSTRY INFLUENCER

BY ALICIA Z. KLEPEIS

Essential Library

An Imprint of Abdo Publishing
abdopublishing.com

Published by Abdo Publishing, a division of ABDO, PO Box 398166, Minneapolis, Minnesota 55439. Copyright © 2018 by Abdo Consulting Group, Inc. International copyrights reserved in all countries. No part of this book may be reproduced in any form without written permission from the publisher. Essential Library™ is a trademark and logo of Abdo Publishing.

Printed in the United States of America, North Mankato, Minnesota
102017
012018

Cover Photo: Prince Williams/WireImage/Getty Images
Interior Photos: Christopher Polk/MTV1415/Getty Images Entertainment/Getty Images, 4, 8–9; Seth Poppel/Yearbook Library, 12, 16; angelonfire CC2.0, 20–21; Everett Collection/Shutterstock Images, 22, 36, 44; Johnny Nunez/WireImage/Getty Images, 26–27; S. Bukley/Shutterstock Images, 30, 32; Tim Klein/Getty Images Entertainment/Getty Images, 38; Theo Wargo/WireImage/Getty Images, 40; Getty Images Entertainment/Getty Images, 47; Reed Saxon/AP Images, 50–51; Kevork Djansezian/AP Images, 53; Michael Kim/AP Images, 57; M. Tran/FilmMagic/Getty Images, 59; Zhu liangcheng/Imaginechina/AP Images, 60; Dominique Charriau/WireImage/Getty Images, 63; Jason DeCrow/AP Images, 66; Chris Pizzello/AP Images, 69; Julio Cortes/AP Images, 70–71; Photofab/Rex Features/AP Images, 73; Marc Piasecki/GC Images/Getty Images, 74; Kevin Mazur/WireImage/Getty Images, 78; Dimitrios Kambouris/Getty Images Entertainment/Getty Images, 81; Debby Wong/Shutterstock Images, 82–83; Shutterstock Images, 85, 96–97; Rob Grabowski/Invision/AP Images, 86; Yui Mok/Press Association/URN:22353135/AP Images, 92–93

Editor: Brenda Haugen
Series Designer: Laura Polzin

PUBLISHER'S CATALOGING-IN-PUBLICATION DATA

Names: Klepeis, Alicia Z., author.
Title: Kanye West: music industry influencer / by Alicia Z. Klepeis.
Other titles: Music industry influencer
Description: Minneapolis, Minnesota : Abdo Publishing, 2018. | Series: Hip-hop artists | Includes online resources and index.
Identifiers: LCCN 2017946876 | ISBN 9781532113307 (lib.bdg.) | ISBN 9781532152184 (ebook)
Subjects: LCSH: West, Kanye, 1977-.--Juvenile literature. | Rap musicians--United States--Biography--Juvenile literature. | Rap (Music)--Juvenile literature.
Classification: DDC 782.421649 [B]--dc23
LC record available at https://lccn.loc.gov/2017946876

CONTENTS

Chapter ONE

KANYE ALWAYS SURPRISES

A crowd of the world's hottest musicians and entertainment celebrities filled the seats of the Microsoft Theater in Los Angeles, California, on August 30, 2015. Some stars were there to perform at the MTV Video Music Awards (VMAs). Others simply wanted to rock out. But Kanye West was there for a special reason. He had been selected to receive the top award of the evening, the Michael Jackson Video Vanguard Award.

Throughout his career, West has used video to express himself both as a musician and as an artist. As MTV said in a statement, "West has blended musical and visual artistry to powerful effect. . . . From his trilogy of videos for 'Jesus Walks' to the mind-bending animation of 'Heartless,' to the arresting imagery of 'Bound 2,' he's pushed boundaries and delivered something new with every successive video."[1]

West soaked in his moment during the 2015 MTV Video Music Awards.

West's fans never know what to expect when one of his new videos is released. He has created more than 40 music videos, including scenes ranging from street battles to dances in cornfields to sexy motorcycle rides. West's music and art never stay the same for long.

Past Vanguard Award winners include Madonna, Michael Jackson, and Beyoncé. MTV gave this award to West in 2015 "for his career spanning groundbreaking videos, legendary VMA performances, and continued impact on music, art, fashion, and culture."[2]

Attendees at the 2015 VMAs were treated to a montage of some of West's videos before he received his award. The sequence of video footage focused on the themes of truth,

FASHION AT THE 2015 VMAS

The VMAs ceremony is one of the most important nights of the year for fashion lovers. In 2015, many attendees wore clothing from some of the world's most famous designers. Rita Ora dazzled in a feathered gown by Vera Wang. Kanye West's wife, Kim Kardashian, wore a long neutral-toned dress from Balmain. Other attendees went for more outrageous outfits. Miley Cyrus's tiny silver ensemble pushed fashion boundaries. So did the colorful pants and shirtless combination of American fashion designer Jeremy Scott. West, though, did not wear a super-slick tuxedo or a suit and tie, nor did he choose flashy clothes that would stand out. Instead, he donned taupe-colored sweatpants and a T-shirt—from his own Yeezy collection, of course.

beauty, and vision, while the narrator shared some commentary about West as an artist.

KANYE WEST AND TAYLOR SWIFT

"The artist aims for perfection. He wants to be the best. . . . When we see his work, we feel this energy. It transforms us."[5]

—Samuel L. Jackson, MTV Video Vanguard presentation, August 30, 2015

Taylor Swift presented the 2015 Video Vanguard Award to West. As she waited to hand him his golden Moonman statue, the mood in the room was electric. The audience gave West a standing ovation. Spotlights brightened the darkness, and the lyrics of West's song "Power" blared through the theater: "Do it better than anybody you ever seen do it/Screams from the haters, got a nice ring to it."[3]

Audience members clapped wildly as West climbed the stairs. The crowd repeatedly chanted, "Kanye! Kanye!"

Many people were surprised that Swift presented West with the award. On September 13, 2009, Swift had just been presented the award for Best Female Video at the VMAs when West rushed onto the stage. He grabbed the microphone from Swift and complained about the decision to give her the award. "I'm sorry, but Beyoncé had one of the best videos of all time!" he proclaimed.[4] He was

speaking about Beyoncé's huge hit "Single Ladies." The audience was stunned. Beyoncé looked mortified as she watched Swift's shocked reaction.

Swift was hurt by West's actions. In an interview with *People* magazine, she said, "I was standing onstage and I was really excited because I'd just won the award, and then I was really excited because Kanye West was onstage. . . . And then I wasn't excited anymore after that."[6] To make matters worse, once West handed the microphone back to Swift, her time to make her acceptance speech had run out.

AN UNUSUAL ACCEPTANCE SPEECH

When most performers receive an award, they spend a minute or two thanking the people who have helped them throughout their careers. But West is not most performers. Once Swift left the stage after giving him his award, West said nothing for close to half a minute. He seemed to

WEST AND AWARD CEREMONIES

West and award ceremonies do not always mix well. On several occasions, he has interrupted other award recipients. Sometimes he did this because he felt he should have won. Other times he believed another nominee deserved the award. Throughout his career, West has often chosen not to attend award ceremonies. He has also admitted to drinking or smoking marijuana before award ceremonies. He was even photographed on the red carpet at the 2009 MTV Awards carrying a bottle of hard liquor. This is not typical or appropriate behavior for musicians attending award ceremonies.

At the 2015 VMAs, West spoke about award ceremonies. He said, "I still don't understand awards shows. I don't understand how they get five people who worked their entire life . . . sold records, sold concert tickets to come stand on the carpet and for the first time in they life be judged on the chopping block and have the opportunity to be considered a loser!"[8]

drink in the adoration of the crowd. Then, he started speaking. While most acceptance speeches are a minute or two long, West spoke for more than 11 minutes. Rather than thanking important people for supporting him, he questioned his own behavior in the past. In front of a group of his peers and fans, he asked, "If I had a daughter at that time would I have went on stage and grabbed the mic from someone else [Taylor]?"[7] He acknowledged that sometimes he had been disrespectful to other artists. But he also discussed how it is important for artists to express their opinions.

As his speech continued, West spoke about his belief in himself. Throughout his career, he has been known for his confidence. In the past, West has called himself "one of the greatest rappers in the world."[9] Based on such statements, many people have considered him arrogant.

But on this night, West used his platform at the VMAs to encourage people to inspire confidence in the next generation: "We gonna teach our kids that they can be something. We not gonna teach low self-esteem and hate to our kids. We gonna teach our kids that they can stand up for theyself! We gonna teach our kids to believe in themselves!"[10] The audience celebrated this positive message.

West could have ended his speech with an expression of gratitude. Instead, West decided to end his speech with a shocker: he announced that he would run for president of the United States in 2020. Stay tuned.

ATLANTA TO CHICAGO

Chapter Two

Kanye Omari West was born on June 8, 1977, in Douglasville, Georgia, approximately 30 minutes away from Atlanta. Kanye's mother, Donda, and father, Ray, wanted him to have a name that was both strong and representative of his culture. *Kanye* is an Ethiopian name meaning "the only one," and *Omari* means "wise man."

Kanye was born into a well-educated family. His mother was an English professor, and his father was a successful photojournalist. Both of Kanye's parents were strong advocates for the rights of African Americans. Kanye grew up thinking and talking about issues of importance to African Americans. This influenced his music as he grew older.

Kanye had a happy childhood.

A LEGACY OF SOCIAL JUSTICE

Social justice was important to both of Kanye's parents. In the 1950s, Donda attended some of the first lunch counter sit-ins in Oklahoma City. The lunch counter sit-ins were a form of nonviolent protest in which people of color asked to be served at white-only lunch counters. When they were refused service, the protesters would continue to sit politely at the counters. Eventually, all people in the United States could eat at any lunch counter they wanted. Through these experiences, Donda had a sense of justice instilled in her. She passed that on to Kanye.

In college, Kanye's father, Ray, had been a member of the Black Panther Party. Founded in California in 1966, this revolutionary party was formed to protect African Americans from acts of police brutality. Ray supported the group's goals of enforcing African-American rights and improving housing, health care, and education for the black community.

MARRIAGE TROUBLES AND A MOVE

Even though Kanye's parents had been in love when they married, their careers took them in different directions. They split up when Kanye was 11 months old and divorced in August 1980. However, Ray and Donda both cared deeply about their son, who would remain an only child. Until he was 15 years old, Kanye spent summers with his dad in Atlanta, Georgia.

Kanye and his mom moved from Atlanta to Chicago, Illinois, when he was three years old. Donda started a new teaching job at Chicago State University. Even as a preschooler,

Kanye showed artistic talent and his own vision of the world. As his mother later recalled, "Even then, his talent stood out. He drew things that kids twice his age couldn't draw."[1] Kanye rarely drew things the color that they actually were in nature. He would make purple bananas and blue oranges. Kanye was bright. He knew which colors the objects were in real life, but he wanted to share his own ideas on paper. That unique artistic vision has stayed with him in just about every creative endeavor he has pursued.

COMFORTING HIS MOTHER

The kitchen of the house on South Shore Drive in Chicago where Kanye lived with his mom for eight years was featured in his song "Hey Mama." Donda had been disappointed in a romantic relationship. Seven-year-old Kanye found his mom with tears in her eyes. At the time, Kanye kneeled on the kitchen floor and told her, "Mama, I'm gonna love you 'til you don't hurt no more."[2] Kanye never forgot that experience.

MUSIC AND YOUNG KANYE

Even though Kanye was smart and artistically gifted, he struggled with interpersonal skills. His preschool teachers said he was self-centered and did not work well with other children. He liked to lead and have his way.

Kanye enjoyed a variety of artistic activities.

Kanye attended Vanderpoel Elementary Magnet School from kindergarten through eighth grade. A magnet school is a public school that offers special programs and instruction not available at all schools. Vanderpoel was focused on teaching the arts.

Even in elementary school, Kanye loved music. His earliest musical idols included Stevie Wonder and Michael Jackson. Kanye also enjoyed the music of George Michael, Madonna, and Phil Collins. Kanye wanted to create music from a young age, but he was not interested in studying music in a formal way, such as taking piano lessons.

Always a fan of being in the spotlight, Kanye often performed in talent shows. When he was seven years old, he practiced lip-syncing for weeks before his performance of Stevie Wonder's "I Just Called to Say I Love You." He wore fake braids and sunglasses to look like Wonder. Kanye felt confident that his act was the best in the show. However, right before Kanye's favorite part of the song, the person running the backing track cut off the music. Kanye was stunned. He went silent and ended up losing the talent show. The loss motivated him, though, and for years after the Stevie Wonder disaster, Kanye won that same talent show over and over again. This helped forge his belief that both talent and hard work should be rewarded in a fair fashion.

Kanye began rapping in third grade. LL Cool J and Run-DMC were among his early influences. Since his mom was a stickler for not using bad language, Kanye had to listen quietly in his room to hear the music of rappers who swore, such as Eazy-E and the Beastie Boys.

RELIGIOUS UPBRINGING

Kanye's parents raised him as a Christian. Kanye regularly attended Sunday school. Even as a young boy, he seemed to have deep beliefs. One afternoon when Kanye was playing, he pointed at the doorway of his Chicago apartment and said, "Look, there goes Jesus."[4] At different times of his life, Kanye has said that angels were with him. The religious lessons Kanye learned as a boy have stayed with him into his adulthood and sometimes make their way into the lyrics of his songs, such as "Jesus Walks."

"I was really raised in the church, and raised as a good Black man."[5]

–Kanye West

ADVENTURES IN CHINA

In 1987, Kanye went with his mom to China for a year. They went there because Donda had a chance to teach in Nanjing as part of the Fulbright Scholar program, a prestigious scholarship that funds Americans to study internationally. It was an eye-opening experience for Kanye. The language, customs, and foods were all new. Even the traffic seemed odd, with bicycles traveling down city streets in droves. It was so different from Chicago.

Kanye rode his bike to a local school and was the only foreigner in the class. Without Chinese language skills, Kanye was put into a first-grade class, even though he was ten years old. He learned quickly, picking up the language and making strides in other subjects such as math and science. Kanye also took private art lessons and tai chi classes.

Kanye stood out in his Chinese school. Kids often stared at him. Some were even bold enough to touch his skin. Kanye later recalled, "It was weird going over there. . . . Most of the kids had never seen a black person before so they'd come over to me and touch my face, thinkin' it was paint or something."[6]

PARENTING KANYE

Kanye's mother, Dr. Donda West, published a book in 2007 titled *Raising Kanye: Life Lessons from the Mother of a Hip-Hop Superstar*. She mentioned how one of her biggest challenges was figuring out how to discipline her creative, opinionated son while also keeping his spirit alive. Making sure Kanye behaved appropriately was also vital to Donda. In her words, "To me, being appropriate does not always mean conforming. Often it means just the opposite. Sometimes, refusing to conform and even confronting is not only appropriate but necessary to change the world for the better."[7]

It was common for the local children to see Kanye and call out, "Break-dance, break-dance!" Instead of growing annoyed with people's stereotypes of him as an American or as a person of color, he used it to his advantage. He started charging people for his break-dance performances

Kanye has continued to draw on lessons from his childhood and teachings from his religious faith throughout his career.

and used the income to buy street food from local vendors.

After a year in China, Kanye and his mother moved back to Chicago. Not too long after his return, Kanye had a run-in with some tough kids in the park behind his house. They wanted the bike he was riding, but Kanye, always

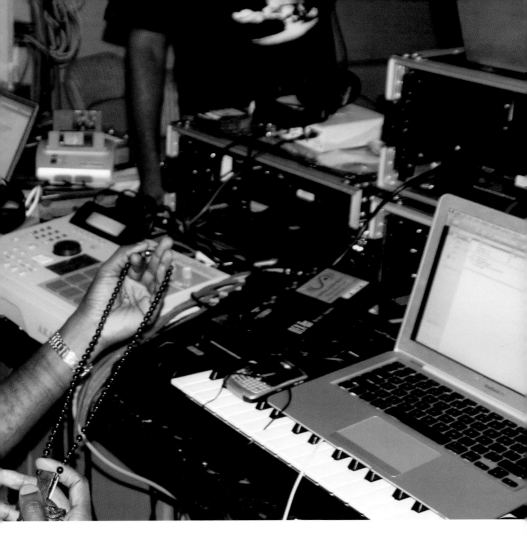

fiercely independent and confident, would not hand it over. As he was riding away, one kid slashed his bike tire with a knife. Donda decided it was time to move. Kanye and his mom settled into a new home in Blue Island, 16 miles (26 km) south of the city. But more than just his address was changing. Kanye was growing up.

KEYBOARDS AND CONTACTS

Art. Music. Fashion. Kanye was passionate about them all during his middle and high school years. By the time he was 11 years old, Kanye took great pride in how he looked and what he wore. Kanye even washed his own laundry to be sure he had exactly what he wanted to wear when he wanted to wear it. He was very particular about brands and styles of clothes. One year, his mother gave him $200 to shop for school clothes. At the time, that would have been enough money to buy a number of complete outfits. Instead, Kanye used the money to purchase upscale items—just one pair of jeans and two shirts.

Kanye also used his flair for fashion to style Quadro Posse, a dance act that he performed with at various talent shows. As Kanye continued to rack up successes in

Kanye has cared about fashion since he was a young child.

such competitions, his confidence grew. He believed he was destined for greatness and would one day be a star.

Kanye roamed down the school hallways, rapping to himself—spitting lyrics he had created on his own. He was just 13 years old when he recorded his first rap. It was named after the Dr. Seuss book *Green Eggs and Ham*. It took some time to find a recording studio that was affordable, but Kanye never gave up when he wanted something badly enough. His mother agreed to pay for the recording. Kanye's long and remarkable recording career had begun.

> "I loved writing raps too much. Rap was the best way to express what was on my mind."[1]
> —Kanye West

FROM CREATING VIDEO GAMES TO MAKING MUSIC

In seventh grade, Kanye wanted to design video games, so he got an Amiga computer with a variety of graphics programs. He had an eye for design and was excited about the 4,096 colors he had to choose from on the computer. He started bringing the ideas for his video games to life, making the graphics himself.

Although Kanye first focused on designing video games, the way he used the computer soon changed. He started creating beats for his video games. Beats are the background over which an artist can rap or sing a new tune. Kanye was hooked, and soon making music was where he put all of his energy. He tells a story about himself from this era: "I found myself running home to use this sound program. . . . It's how I learned to produce. In seventh grade."[2] The program allowed Kanye to record one note at a time until he had a combination of notes or a melody he liked.

Kanye wanted desperately to record and produce his own music at home. He saved his money, hoping to purchase a professional-quality keyboard. Donda recognized how motivated Kanye was, so for Christmas in 1991, she pitched in $1,000 toward his equipment fund. Kanye immediately started working on beats on his new keyboard.

> "I thought I was going to get signed back when I was 13 years old."[3]
>
> –Kanye West

While other kids his age were studying or hanging out with their friends, Kanye spent most of his time working to develop his craft. It wasn't that he was antisocial.

Friends came over, and they would listen to the newest records together. They checked out hip-hop albums, such as *The Low End Theory* by A Tribe Called Quest. They also enjoyed hearing rap albums by Run-DMC, Public Enemy, and the Wu-Tang Clan. Kanye's parents were not always thrilled with rap and hip-hop music. The songs in these genres often talked about violence and bad behavior. Sometimes the lyrics were insulting to women and African Americans. Regardless of his parents' objections, Kanye was a huge rap fan. He even started his own rap group when he was 13. It was called State of Mind, and it was made up of Kanye and two of his friends.

MAKING CONNECTIONS IN HIGH SCHOOL

Kanye started attending Polaris High School in Oak Lawn, Illinois, in the fall of 1991. He gradually acquired more recording equipment and put together his own studio

FIRST JOBS

As a teen, Kanye worked various jobs to supplement his allowance. He cut hair in a barbershop. He traveled door-to-door selling knives but decided that was not really his thing. He also worked as a greeter at the Gap. Kanye put his own spin on the greeting job, choosing to freestyle as people entered the store: "Welcome to the Gap/We got jeans in the back/ And we got some khaki slacks."[4]

at home with a keyboard, turntable, and mixer. He spent most of his time in his bedroom working on his beats. It was during high school that Kanye met one of the most important figures in his early musical life: No I.D.

No I.D. was a DJ and music producer in Chicago. He was six years older than Kanye and was known for his work with Common, a Chicago-based rapper. Kanye was just 14 years old when he and No I.D. met. No I.D.'s mom worked at Chicago State University, where Kanye's mother taught. Donda asked No I.D.'s mother if she could convince her son to speak with Kanye and help him break into the music business. Kanye wanted to learn everything he could from the older and wiser producer. He would pester No I.D., even camping out in his driveway until No I.D. returned from wherever he'd been. No I.D. recalled their early interactions, saying, "He [Kanye] was just one of them energetic kids, like 'Teach me everything, teach me anything!' At first it was just like 'All right man, take this, learn this, go, get, get, get.' But eventually he started getting good. He was always trying to prove himself, and he kept getting better and better."[5] No I.D. taught Kanye how to sample music. He also taught him how to record over samples when making his own musical creations.

At 14, Kanye also began cutting hair in a barbershop. When he was 16 years old, Kanye met the rapper GLC. They met through a friend of GLC's who had gotten his hair cut by Kanye. The friend brought GLC to Kanye's home to introduce the two. GLC and Kanye started making songs together right away. GLC noticed how serious Kanye was about his work. As Kanye continued through high school, his grades dropped, but he gained experience and local recognition for his skills as a producer and rapper.

WHAT IS SAMPLING?

Music sampling is a popular practice in hip-hop music. Sampling is a form of musical borrowing whereby a musical artist incorporates a track from an already-recorded song into a brand new one. An artist might sample the drums of a song or just some of the vocals. Sometimes artists sample more than one song at a time within their new piece. Artists who sample from other musicians' music must pay to use the original work. In his earliest days of sampling, Kanye sampled the music of artists such as Luther Vandross and Michael Jackson, among others.

DeRay Davis was among the first to recognize Kanye's gifts as a rapper.

When given the chance to show his stuff to DeRay Davis, an actor and comedian who had connections to the rap group Def Squad, Kanye was on fire. He rapped nonstop for half an hour. Davis said, "The dude [Kanye] did not stop spitting. . . . He probably did a whole album back to back. I'm literally like, 'Yo, this kid is crazy.'"[6] How far could Kanye go? No one knew. But his career in music had definitely begun.

"Kanye applied himself. . . . That dude was focused since he was a shorty [a kid]."[7]

–Rapper GLC

SUCCESS, REJECTION, AND DROPPING OUT

Kanye entered a number of national-level art contests during high school—and won every one. He graduated from Polaris High School in 1995. With a college professor for a mother, Kanye was strongly encouraged to get a higher degree. He was told that art might be a good avenue for his future education. While he sorted out his next academic step, Kanye kept working on his music.

One of his earliest successes involved a Chicago-based rapper called Gravity, or Grav. In an interview, Grav told the story of when he first met Kanye. Grav said he was either coming out of or going into a Fugees concert when Kanye ran up to him. Kanye said, "Yo, I heard you got a record deal. Yo, you should let me get some beats on your album. I'm nice. I got skills. You should just come to the

Kanye never worried about fitting rap star stereotypes.

car and let me play some beats for you."[1] Gravity agreed and listened to the cassette Kanye popped into the player of his car. Grav was impressed. "Fire. Fire, off the bat. I'm telling you, the boy was a child prodigy way back then," he recalled.[2]

Grav and his record label loved Kanye's beats. Grav bought Kanye's earliest professional beats from him for $8,800. Kanye used the money to buy Polo brand clothes and a piece of jewelry featuring Jesus. Kanye was investing in his own unique look, trying to carve out a niche in the hip-hop scene.

Kanye produced eight tracks on Grav's 1996 debut album, *Down to Earth*. The album earned many good reviews. People commented on how it moved audiences without focusing on materialism, as a lot of rap music did at the time. The *Rap Pages* December 1996 review said, "DOWN TO EARTH gives you that

GUEST RAPPER

Kanye was an essential figure on Grav's *Down to Earth* album. As a producer on eight tracks of the album, Kanye was able to create another opportunity for himself: the chance to do a guest appearance as a rapper on the song "Line for Line." Kanye's voice was sharp and acidic as he spit lyrics that were critical of the gangsta lifestyle and ambitions. He talked about crazy men dreaming of having a Lexus and coupés and finished his verse with "Kill the black-on-black crime."[3]

genuine dirty-yet-phat street sound that true Hip-Hop listeners have grown to cherish."[4]

THE STING OF REJECTION

Kanye was beginning to make a name for himself, so he was beyond excited when Columbia Records contacted him. It was the summer just after his nineteenth birthday. Columbia Records rolled out the red carpet for the young producer. They flew him from Chicago to New York and picked him up from the airport in a limousine.

Always confident, Kanye was sure he would leave New York with a recording contract. He was cocky when interacting with the people at Columbia. He boasted that he was going to be a big musical star like Michael Jackson. Kanye said he would be better than Atlanta-based producer Jermaine Dupri. These were pretty outrageous claims for a relative newcomer to the hip-hop scene.

Michael Mauldin, an executive at Columbia, interviewed Kanye, asking what his niche was in music. Kanye could not come up with a good answer. He had failed the test, so to speak. Kanye left the record company offices with a false promise of "We'll call you."[5] Later, Kanye discovered that among the mistakes he made in that interview was his comment about Jermaine Dupri.

Jermaine Dupri continues to be a force in the hip-hop world.

Michael Mauldin was Dupri's father. Kanye headed back to Chicago, more determined than ever to make something of himself.

DROPPING OUT

"When he got back home [from the meeting at Columbia], Kanye . . . was producing music and writing raps like the world was coming to an end."[6]

—*Donda West*

In addition to working on his music, Kanye started attending the American Academy of Art in Chicago in 1997 because it offered classes in fashion and interior design. Kanye studied there for a semester and learned about painting. But he did not like having to draw what someone else told him to draw, and he did not want to pursue the fine arts. Kanye switched colleges and began attending Chicago State University, which was where his mother taught. Donda soon heard that Kanye was not regularly attending his classes there.

Education was important to both of Kanye's parents. But Kanye was not satisfied with college. He wanted to work on his music, not do assignments for professors. In 1998, 20-year-old Kanye dropped out of Chicago State. Kanye's mother was not thrilled with his decision, but she knew how passionate her son was about music. She told him to take a year and see whether he could make his musical dreams come true.

"SPACESHIP"

The song "Spaceship," from Kanye's 2004 album *The College Dropout*, focuses on this period of Kanye's life. In the song, he complains about a job at the Gap where people ask him about khakis. He accuses the store of using him as a greeter to make it seem diverse: "I bet they show off their token blackie/Oh, now they love Kanye, let's put him all in the front of the store."[7] The lyrics to this song also reference how Kanye would lock himself in a room at home, making several beats a day over the course of three summers. His frustration was clear on this track, which features rappers GLC and Consequence, as well as a sample from Marvin Gaye's song "Distant Lover."

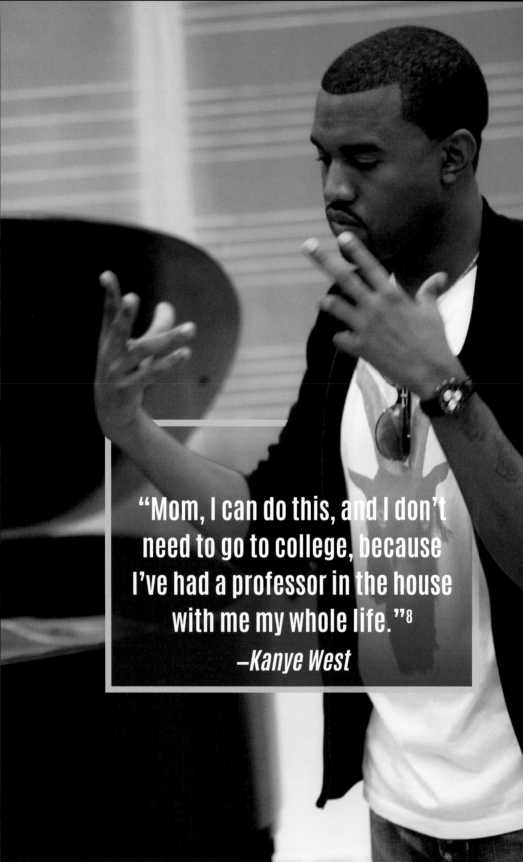

"Mom, I can do this, and I don't need to go to college, because I've had a professor in the house with me my whole life."[8]
–Kanye West

It was not a free ride for Kanye. Donda charged Kanye rent, so in addition to working on his musical projects, Kanye had to earn cash. He lasted just one day as a busboy at a restaurant. He worked as a telemarketing salesperson, too. Kanye knew how to chat with people and was persuasive with customers, so he had some success as a telemarketer. After working all day, he stayed up late at night to develop his production and rapping skills. He also made beats to sell to other rappers and hip-hop artists, such as Ma$e. But even Kanye might not have predicted the number of amazing musical collaborations that lay just around the corner for him.

TELEMARKETING TROUBLES

Kanye had a couple of telemarketing jobs after dropping out of college. Even though he was quite good at this type of work, he sometimes quit for odd reasons. One time he quit because his boss told him he could not doodle while talking on the phone. Kanye also did not appreciate it when his supervisor kept calling him the wrong name, saying, "Kanyee, Kanyah, whatever yo name is!"[9] Despite being a smooth talker, Kanye found that telemarketing was not for him.

THE PRODUCER

West's beats were catching the attention of many well-respected people in the music industry. Among them was producer Jermaine Dupri. Dupri asked West if he would like to contribute to his album *Jermaine Dupri Presents Life in 1472: The Original Soundtrack*. West accepted the invitation and ended up producing the song "(Intro) Turn It Out." Producing the song was also exciting because West got to work with Nas, one of his rapper heroes.

Dupri's album was released in July 1998 and went platinum. With a beat on such a successful album, West's star was really starting to shine. Many artists asked to collaborate with him, including Foxy Brown, Harlem World, and Lil' Kim.

Through these collaborations, West was able to showcase his musical range as a producer. For example, West produced six tracks on *Tell 'Em Why U Madd* by the Madd Rapper. The tracks vary widely in feel and style. "Ghetto" talks about Beverly Hills and wearing "Polo" and features piano blinging. "You're All Alone" focuses

West's first time working with his idol Nas would not be his last.

on street violence and weapons and has a funky sound with drums. West's name appeared on some of the most celebrated hip-hop albums of the late 1990s.

GO GETTERS

Kanye was part of a rap group called the Go Getters in the late 1990s. It was made up of Kanye, GLC, Timmy G, and Arrowstar. The group recorded enough music to fill an album. The album was tentatively titled *World Record Holders* and featured several special guests, including Rhymefest, Miss Criss, and Mikkey Halsted. Although the group had promotional photos taken and even made some radio appearances, their album was never released. However, they did have a hit single in 1998 titled "Oh Oh Oh," which had a style compared to that of Snoop Dogg. The subject matter of the song, including mistreating a woman and kidnapping someone at gunpoint, is not typical of later Kanye tunes.

GETTING STARTED WITH ROC-A-FELLA

No I.D. continued to help West by calling attention to his young protégé among his contacts at various record companies. People at Roc-A-Fella Records invited West to do a trial track for Beanie Sigel's first album, *The Truth*. This was a chance for the folks at Roc-A-Fella to see if they liked working with West. West ended up producing the title track for Sigel's album. It had a dark feel to it and included a sample from "Chicago," a song by Graham Nash.

West was still living in Chicago, but his year of trying to make it as a hip-hop artist was over. Donda was tired of her son being loud and inviting a constant parade of people to her house. Kanye moved out. By selling beats to local artists and doing production work, he barely scraped by. Then West came up with a beat that was his ticket to the big time. It included a sample from the song "I Miss You" by Harold Melvin & The Blue Notes. West played it over the phone to Roc-A-Fella employee Kyambo "Hip-Hop" Joshua, who loved it. West sent a copy to Joshua in New York. When rap superstar Jay-Z heard the beat, he also thought it was great. Jay-Z had co-founded Roc-A-Fella in 1995 and worked with Joshua on various projects. West was given a huge opportunity: to produce the track "This Can't Be Life" on Jay-Z's album *The Dynasty: Roc la Familia*. Kanye was starstruck at getting to collaborate with another of his heroes.

ROC-A-FELLA RECORDS

Roc-A-Fella Records is one of the most famous hip-hop and rap record labels in the world. Based in New York City, it was founded in 1995 by Jay-Z, Damon Dash, and Kareem "Biggs" Burke. Some of the biggest names in rap and hip-hop have recorded their albums on this label. In addition to Kanye West and Jay-Z, other Roc-A-Fella artists have included Memphis Bleek, Beanie Sigel, Cam'ron, Freeway, and Foxy Brown.

West and Jay-Z eventually became friends as well as colleagues.

West worked on more Roc-A-Fella projects, producing two songs on Beanie Sigel's 2001 album, *The Reason*. Perhaps the most important collaboration in West's early career was when he produced several songs on Jay-Z's September 2001 album, *The Blueprint*. The album rose to Number 1 on the Billboard 200 chart. Highly successful songs on the album include "Izzo (H.O.V.A.)" and "Girls,

Girls, Girls." The success of *The Blueprint* launched Kanye further into his career as a producer.

KANYE WANTS TO RAP

West was in demand in the hip-hop production scene, but he still wanted to rap. Since he had connections at Roc-A-Fella Records, he asked the record label's staff to give him a shot. He was allowed to rap a few lines on some songs for other artists, but that was it. West was not satisfied. He wanted to make his own album.

West shopped his work around, meeting with executives at a number of labels, including Arista Records and Def Jam. West came close at Capitol Records, working with an A&R representative known as 3H, but at the last minute, the company pulled out and did not offer him a contract. West was beyond frustrated. He said, "No joke— I'd leave meetings crying all the time."[1]

Today it may seem strange that no one wanted to give West a contract to rap, but at the time, some music industry representatives did not think he was that talented as a rapper. Others questioned his middle-class upbringing. Some companies, including Roc-A-Fella, wondered if fans would want to hear music from a guy who did not have a tough life. He was not selling drugs.

He was not involved with street violence. As Jay-Z noted, "We all grew up street guys who had to do whatever we had to do to get by. Then there's Kanye, who to my knowledge has never hustled a day in his life. I didn't see how it could work."[2]

Another strike against West was his unique fashion style. West did not fit the profile of a typical rapper. Damon Dash, the former CEO of Roc-A-Fella, recalled Kanye wearing a pink shirt and Gucci loafers. He said, "It was obvious we were not from the same place or cut from the same cloth."[3]

NEAR-DEATH EXPERIENCE

West was busy in a recording studio in Los Angeles, working into the wee hours alongside Ludacris, 3H, and DJ Whoo Kid. He was constantly traveling and producing for a number of well-known artists. In the early morning on October 23, 2002, an exhausted West fell asleep at the wheel on the way back to his hotel. The Lexus West was driving flipped over after it crashed into an oncoming car. Because the airbag did not deploy, West's face hit the steering wheel, breaking his jaw in three places.

Donda later described seeing her son in the hospital: "Kanye was unrecognizable . . . his head was three times its normal size. It was as big as the pillow they had it on. If I had not known I was looking at my own child, I would not have recognized him."[4]

West stayed in the hospital for two weeks. Thinking about music was part of his healing process. He even convinced Damon Dash to bring a drum machine so he could work in bed. West also came to a number of important realizations during his time in the hospital. He felt as though he had been spared through God's

West joined Damon Dash at a party to promote Dash's clothing line in 2002.

TREATMENT AFTER THE ACCIDENT

West has questioned some of the ways he was treated right after his car crash. Despite his trouble breathing and obvious distress due to his injuries, his blood alcohol levels were tested three times. He recalled being asked lots of questions before being pulled from the car: "I just kept telling them [emergency responders], 'I want to go to the hospital, I'm in so much pain right now.'"[6] He had to wait hours to be treated. West seemed convinced this poor treatment was the result of his being a black man.

grace and that angels were looking out for him. In his song "Never Let Me Down," Kanye mentions this belief: "I know I got angels watchin' me from the other side."[5] West also realized he had been spending most of his time working on other people's music instead of his own. He decided to get down to business on his own projects.

As soon as West got out of the hospital, he pleaded with Roc-A-Fella to let him go into the studio to record the track he had been imagining. Despite being on painkillers and having his jaw wired shut for an additional month after being released from the hospital, West managed to record his song "Through the Wire." Listeners can hear the strain in his voice as he raps without being able to open his mouth all the way.

The lyrics of "Through the Wire" cover a wide range of topics. In one line West compares his post-injury appearance to that of Emmett Till, a 14-year-old African-American boy who was brutally murdered in 1955. But West also expresses gratitude, saying, "Thank God I ain't too cool for the safe belt."[7]

When West recorded "Through the Wire," he still did not have a record deal. He put the song on a mixtape, which he shared with record executives in yet another effort to get a recording contract. Finally, Roc-A-Fella offered him a deal. At last West would be able to make an album of his own.

SNUBBED AT MADISON SQUARE GARDEN

Several Roc-A-Fella artists were going to perform at Madison Square Garden in New York City in November 2003. West asked if he could perform along with the other musicians, but his request was denied. He was just given two free tickets to see the show.

West decided not to attend, choosing to work on his own music in the studio instead. "Next year, I'll have my own show at Madison Square Garden!" West predicted.[8] And he did—as the opening act for Usher.

Chapter SIX

HIGHLIGHTS AND LOW LIGHTS

Kanye's debut album, *The College Dropout*, was released on February 10, 2004. It was innovative and unique, showcasing West's rapping and genius production skills. Critics were fascinated by the album's diverse collection of songs. *Billboard* said, "'The College Dropout' was the voice of levity. The voice of a dreamer. The voice of someone who nobody took seriously."[1]

Unlike many hip-hop artists of the time, West did not just rap about violence on the city streets or the material items money could buy. His skits "Workout Plan" and "The New Workout Plan" show a comedic, satirical side to the album. With its religious focus, "Jesus Walks" expanded the boundaries of hip-hop lyrical content.

West also collaborated with many celebrated musicians on *The College Dropout*, including Ludacris, Jay-Z, and Talib Kweli. West's track "Slow Jamz," featuring

West won his first Grammy Awards in 2005.

HIP-HOP SKITS

Since he was a teenager, Kanye took inspiration from hip-hop skits. Made popular by De La Soul and Prince Paul, these skits were like an artistic glue linking songs on an album. Hip-hop skits are recorded sketches that serve as interludes on an album. Often comedic, they are frequently written and performed by the artist him - or herself. The skits of the Wu-Tang Clan, for instance, could be funny or angry, featuring stream-of-consciousness talking or even sound effects such as gunshots. Producer Prince Paul said he used such skits "to fill that void, to give our album some structure. . . . We never thought it would become a rap album staple."[4] Kanye said the skits of the Wu-Tang Clan had a big impact on his music and the genre of rap. Kanye used skits on some of his own albums.

"That record [*The College Dropout*] restored my faith in hip-hop."[5]
—Actor and Musician Jamie Foxx

Twista and Jamie Foxx, rocketed up the charts to Number 1.

The College Dropout was a huge success. It sold more than 400,000 copies in its first week.[2] In total, the album sold more than three million copies. As the *New York Times* stated, "Throughout the album Mr. West taunts everyone who didn't believe in him: teachers, record executives, police officers, even his former boss at the Gap."[3]

THE 2005 GRAMMYS

The forty-seventh annual Grammy Awards were held at the Staples Center in Los Angeles on February 13, 2005. For West, this would be a night to remember.

Before the festivities even began, West could walk in proud. He had been nominated for ten Grammys—more than any other artist. Part of the reason West was nominated so many times was his involvement with music on so many levels—as a producer, songwriter, and performer.

On this special night, West also performed in front of a packed audience. His unforgettable rendition of "Jesus

West performed "Jesus Walks" at the 2005 Grammy Awards.

Walks" took place on a stage with an elaborate set featuring a church backdrop with fake stained-glass windows and a full gospel choir. The performance ended with West wearing a white suit with feathered angel wings.

That night West won three Grammy Awards: Best Rap Album for *The College Dropout*, Best Rap Song for "Jesus Walks," and a win for his songwriting on Alicia Keys's "You Don't Know My Name." West's acceptance speech for the Best Rap Album moved many people. He mentioned his 2002 accident, saying, "If you have the opportunity to play this game of life, you need to appreciate every moment."[6] And, in classic West fashion, he gave a shout-out to those who doubted him, saying, "Everybody wanted to know what I would do if I didn't win. I guess we'll never know."[7]

THE LOUIS VUITTON DON

West has been a huge fan of high-end French designer Louis Vuitton (LV) for a long time. In his 2004 song "Last Call," West refers to himself as "Kan, the Louis Vuitton Don."[8] After the release of *The College Dropout*, West often sported an LV backpack. When West turned 30, he held his over-the-top birthday bash at the Louis Vuitton store in New York. Guests included John Legend, Jay-Z, Rihanna, and Sean Combs, among others. In conjunction with Louis Vuitton, West launched a collection of men's shoes known as the Louis Vuitton Don in 2009.

ON TOP OF THE WORLD

West's career was on fire. His music was playing on the radio, and his videos were on television. His second album, *Late Registration*, dropped on August 30, 2005. It went over its production budget, costing a whopping $2 million to make.[9] It contained 21 tracks and included collaborations with Maroon 5 singer Adam Levine on "Heard 'Em Say," as well as rappers Common, Nas, and Jay-Z. West's song "Gold Digger" featured Jamie Foxx and was a huge hit, spending ten weeks at the top of the *Billboard* Hot 100.

Just before the album's release, West talked about his new record: "I wanted to make something that's never been heard before."[10] He hired Jon Brion as coproducer on the album. Brion was known for producing artsy albums and quirky movie soundtracks. The songs on *Late Registration* include a wide diversity of influences and sounds, from homemade percussion instruments to 24-piece orchestras to vocals by R&B artist Brandy.

In its first week, *Late Registration* sold

> "In Kanye's mind, this is not a crazy art record. He just wanted a different palette of sounds than everyone else in hip-hop. . . . He wants to make music for the entire planet."[11]
>
> –Jon Brion

CHIPMUNK SOUL

One of the signature styles of sampling West is known for is called "chipmunk soul." It got the name because when Kanye speeds up a sample before using it in a song, the sample can sound more like the high-pitched voice of a chipmunk than the deep tones of a soul artist. A prime example of this is his sample of Chaka Khan's song "Through the Fire," which he used on his own track "Through the Wire." After *The College Dropout* came out, many other musicians started to copy West's signature style. This motivated West to move on and begin experimenting with other sampling techniques.

860,000 copies.[12] *Rolling Stone* magazine called *Late Registration* the best album of 2005. Within weeks of its release, the album made it to the top of the *Billboard* 200 chart. It also earned eight Grammy nominations, including Album of the Year. On February 8, 2006, West won three Grammys: Best Rap Album for *Late Registration*, Best Rap Solo Performance for "Gold Digger," and Best Rap Song for "Diamonds (Are from Sierra Leone)."

West released his third album, *Graduation*, on September 11, 2007. *New York Times* writer Jon Caramanica called it "his most eclectic album, drawing on a wide musical palette, including classic rock and dance music."[13] On his single "Stronger," West samples from Daft Punk, a DJ duo from France that was not yet well known. The track

West promoted *Late Registration* on *Good Morning America* just days after the album's release.

"Homecoming" features Coldplay front man Chris Martin, as well as some piano jamming.

As is typical with West's albums, *Graduation*'s subject matter varies widely from track to track. "Big Brother" is a tribute to his friend and mentor Jay-Z. Writers for the website *Complex* called his song "Can't Tell Me Nothing" West's "first true street anthem."[14] The track celebrates the tough attitude of city dwellers. It also showcases the value in urban culture of money, status-laden jewelry,

BATTLE WITH 50 CENT

Both Kanye West and rapper 50 Cent were scheduled to have albums coming out during the summer of 2007. 50 Cent made this into a challenge, saying he would quit recording if West's *Graduation* album sold more copies. West eventually decided to release his album on the same day as 50 Cent's—September 11, 2007. West won the challenge. *Graduation* sold 957,000 copies in its first six days. 50 Cent's album *Curtis* sold 691,000 copies in that same time period.[15] For the record, 50 Cent did not quit recording after losing the challenge. His next album came out in 2009.

and designer clothing. Some critics did not think *Graduation* hung together as well as West's earlier albums. But despite any negative reviews *Graduation* might have gotten, it was a smash hit.

A DEVASTATING LOSS

In 2004, Donda West retired so that she could work with her son. She chaired the Kanye West Foundation, a nonprofit organization aimed at improving literacy and reducing dropout rates. In May 2007, she also published a book about raising her superstar son. Six months later, on November 10, Donda died after elective cosmetic surgery.

Donda had been told to seek advice before having the surgery due to concerns about her heart, but she did not follow this advice. She also left the hospital right after surgery, wanting to recuperate at home. She died the next

West joined his mother at her book signing in Westwood, California, in 2007.

day. Years later, Kanye felt that he was partly to blame for his mother's death. Donda had wanted to look better when going out in public with him. In an interview, he said, "If I had never moved to L.A. she'd be alive. . . . I don't want to go far into it because it will bring me to tears."[16] Just when everything was going so well, West lost the person closest to him. He was gutted.

HEALING AND LOVE

The unexpected death of his beloved mother shook up West's life. She had always been his biggest supporter. But he did his best to keep going, and in April 2008, West performed in venues from Brussels, Belgium, to Seattle, Washington, as part of his Glow in the Dark tour.

One thing that likely boosted West's spirits was his raging success at the 2008 Grammy Awards. He was nominated for eight Grammys and won four: Best Rap Performance by a Duo or Group for "Southside" (a collaboration with Common), Best Rap Song for "Good Times," Best Rap Solo Performance for "Stronger," and Best Rap Album for *Graduation*.

In his acceptance speech, West spoke about hip-hop: "A lot of people said hip-hop was dead. . . . A lot of people just said the art form wasn't popping anymore. I wanted to cross the genres and show people how we

West kept busy performing in 2008.

could still express ourselves with something fresh and new and that's what hip-hop's always been about."[1] West also told the Grammy audience how he appreciated all of the support and prayers he received following his mother's death.

In April 2008, West split up with his fiancée, fashion designer Alexis Phifer. The two had been dating since 2002 and had been engaged since August 2006. In an interview following the breakup, Phifer said, "It's always sad when things like this end, and we remain friends. . . . I wish him the best in his future and all of his endeavors. He's one of the most talented people I've ever met."[2]

808s & HEARTBREAK

One of the ways West endured these tough times was through his music. He went to Hawaii and spent three weeks recording his new album, *808s & Heartbreak*. West

A TRIBUTE TO DONDA

West's song "Hey Mama" on his *Late Registration* album was written as a celebration of the many things Donda did for Kanye when he was growing up. After his mother's death, West began playing the song at his concerts. He also sang a special version of the song with lyrics he updated for the event at the 2008 Grammy Awards. He had the word *MAMA* cut into his hair for the occasion as well.

West and Phifer attended a fashion show in Paris the month before they broke up.

wanted this album to feel different from his previous albums. Not surprisingly, a major theme of *808s & Heartbreak* was loneliness.

The album was a departure from his previous albums in several ways. For one thing, West used an Auto-Tune machine to alter his voice. This album also did not feature nearly as many guest collaborators as in the past. Producer Mike Dean said West had a number of rules when creating the album. Each song had to have an 808 drum pattern in it. West also did not want to use typical hip-hop beats

WHAT'S AN 808?

The Roland TR-808, also known as the 808 drum machine, is an essential piece of equipment in West's music. This machine began influencing the sound of music in the 1980s and quickly became vital to hip-hop musicians. Artists such as West use the 808 to add texture to their music. Musical texture has to do with the number of layers that are used in a composition. For example, a Kanye West track might have sounds from a drum machine as one layer, a sample of another song as a second layer, and then the vocals of West himself on top of these other layers. Producer Arthur Baker described this device: "You didn't know it [the 808 machine] was there, and then it would just blow up a speaker."[4]

on its tracks. He did not rap on the album's songs, such as "Love Lockdown," but sang instead.

808s & Heartbreak was released on November 24, 2008. It did not sell as well as West's previous albums. People had strong opinions about this work. While rapper Common loved it, other critics' opinions were not so favorable. Writer Jeff Weiss said, "The conservative rap diehards that West rode in with are probably going to want to pelt him with rotten grapefruit."[3]

TAKING A BREAK

Between touring and recording, West had kept up a hectic pace. After his drama with Taylor Swift at the September 2009 MTV VMAs, he received a lot of hate from the press and his peers. Jay-Z told West that he thought his behavior was rude and inappropriate. Rock star Pink tweeted about the incident, saying, "Kanye West is the biggest piece of s*** on earth. Quote me."[5]

> "You can't judge me on this [*808s & Heartbreak*] because it's a reflection of my heart and soul. It's like judging a grandmother's love."[6]
>
> *–Kanye West*

Following the advice of friend and fellow hip-hop artist Mos Def, West decided to take a break. He wanted to escape from everyone, including the paparazzi. West was supposed to go on tour in late 2009 with Lady Gaga, but he pulled out without any explanation.

West traveled during his self-imposed time off. First he went to Japan, where he holed up in the famous Grand Hyatt Hotel in Tokyo. He headed to Rome, Italy, in November 2009. He stayed there for several months, not making music for the first time he could remember. West did an internship with the Italian designer Fendi while he was in Italy. As an intern, rather than being waited on and treated like a celebrity, West worked regular hours getting people coffee, photocopying papers, and doing other office chores. He also spent several months living in Hawaii after his time in Europe.

West took the microphone from Swift as she accepted the Best Female Video award during the 2009 VMAs.

During this time when West was largely staying out of the limelight, his work was being celebrated by the music industry. He did not appear at the 2010 Grammy Awards, held on January 31, 2010, but he won two Grammys (Best Rap Song and Best Rap/Sung Collaboration) for

"Run This Town," his collaborative work with Jay-Z and Rihanna.

KANYE'S FANTASY

Eventually West returned to making music. His fifth album, *My Beautiful Dark Twisted Fantasy,* was released on November 22, 2010. The album has a reflective nature. It includes many of the different kinds of sounds found on earlier albums—orchestration as on *Late Registration,* soul samples as on *The College Dropout,* and melodies created using Auto-Tune devices as on *808s & Heartbreak.* In an interview, West said of *My Beautiful Dark Twisted Fantasy,* "It was kind of piecing together what people liked about me to make a bouquet of what people loved."[7]

The album was well received by the critics. The first single from the album was "Power." Music writer Ryan Dombal commented that this song made him think West

THE ROSEWOOD MOVEMENT

West has always been a risk-taker when it comes to fashion. He has never been afraid to stand out. During the summer of 2010, West tried something new, what became known as the Rosewood movement. During this fashion phase, West wore designer suits and ties. He felt this was a classy, elegant look. But the Rosewood movement went beyond just dressing smart. West said it involved not swearing much, "taking care of kids," and "calling your grandmother."[8] The Rosewood movement did not last very long in West's life.

> "*Dark Fantasy* to me is . . . almost like, an apology record."[9]
>
> –Kanye West

had been trapped in a cardboard box for years and now had something to say to the world. The track "All of the Lights" involved 42 people in its making, including pop music king Elton John playing piano. The other instruments featured include drums, woodwinds, and cello. The subject matter covered in "All of the Lights" ranges from a tribute to Michael Jackson to domestic abuse to a celebration of the high life as a celebrity.

WATCH THE THRONE

West and Jay-Z collaborated again, dropping the album *Watch the Throne* on August 8, 2011. The two artists decided to go by the name the Throne rather than their usual names. Both performers were given equal billing.

That does not mean the process of creating the album was all smooth sailing. Both performers have sizable egos. They got into heated arguments over the direction specific tracks and the album as a whole should take. However, the album does not come across as a competition. The megastar artists sometimes rap back and forth within a single track.

West directed the short film "Runaway," which accompanied his album *My Beautiful Dark Twisted Fantasy*.

Watch the Throne addresses social issues, too. For example, the lyrics of the song "Murder to Excellence" make reference to wealthy African-American celebrities

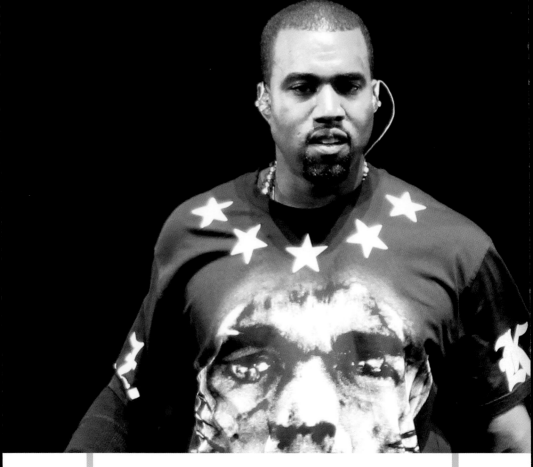

West and Jay-Z went on tour together to promote their album *Watch the Throne.*

Will Smith and Oprah Winfrey: "Only spot a few blacks the higher up I go/What's up to Will, shout-out to O." Another powerful line from "Murder to Excellence" goes as follows: "In the past if you picture events like a black tie/What's the last thing you expect to see? Black guys."[10]

At the 2012 Grammys, the Throne won a Best Rap
Performance Award for the single "Otis." West also
won three other Grammys that night, out of seven
nominations: Best Rap Song and Best Rap Collaboration

West and Kardashian enjoyed a night out in London in November 2012.

for "All of the Lights" and Best Rap Album for *My Beautiful Dark Twisted Fantasy*. He was back in the game.

KANYE AND KIM

With his career soaring, West's love life also took a turn for the better. West started dating reality TV star Kim Kardashian in 2012. They first met in 2004 when she was married to music producer Damon Thomas. West went public about his relationship with Kardashian in June 2012, tweeting about her as his girlfriend.

Their relationship seemed to be on the fast track. In December 2012, West announced they were expecting a baby. Daughter North West was born on June 15, 2013. Life was moving ahead for West, one happy step at a time.

WATCH THE THRONE TOUR

In addition to collaborating on their *Watch the Throne* album, Kanye and Jay-Z also toured together. Starting in Atlanta and ending in Birmingham, England, they did 57 shows between October 28, 2011, and June 22, 2012. The live show was exciting, with much to take in visually, including footage of sharks and Rottweilers. The performers rose on hydraulic cubes at the two ends of the arena. Fans were even treated to a dramatic video-laser ball of fire extravaganza. Promotional T-shirts for the album, designed by Givenchy, cost $300.[11]

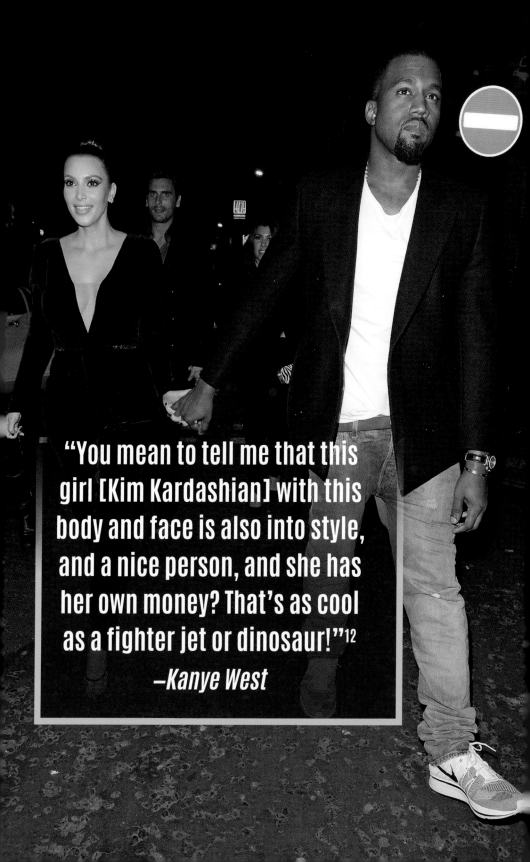

"You mean to tell me that this girl [Kim Kardashian] with this body and face is also into style, and a nice person, and she has her own money? That's as cool as a fighter jet or dinosaur!"[12]
—Kanye West

BEATLES AND BABIES

On June 18, just three days after his daughter North was born, West's next album dropped. Titled *Yeezus*, there have been debates about the origin of the name. Some say it is a combination of West's nickname Yeezy and the name Jesus. Others just find it sacrilegious. After all, Kanye has said some outrageous things about his connection to religion, including "I am God's vessel" and "I'm the closest that hip-hop is getting to God."[1]

Regardless of the controversial title, *Yeezus* captured the attention of the music world. West said the album was not made for radio play. It features a rather jolting production style. West also cut back on samples that might be considered more "pop friendly." Music critic Jon Pareles describes the tracks on *Yeezus* as "raw and bumpy" and mentions the anger West shows in a number

West quickly settled into fatherhood.

of the album's songs, such as "New Slaves" and "Black Skinhead."[2]

Despite the raw feel of *Yeezus*, the album was well received for continuing West's trend of musical innovation. The track "Blood on the Leaves" is a fascinating example of this. In addition to showcasing a wide array of musical instruments, the track also employs an unusual technique—a call-and-response with West's own voice. Perhaps writer Lou Reed summed up the critics' divergent opinions in saying, "There are moments of supreme beauty and greatness on this record [*Yeezus*], and then some of it is the same old [stuff]. But the guy really, really,

THE *YEEZUS* TOUR

West began his *Yeezus* tour in 2013. Night after night, he would perform his new song "Runaway" and then treat fans to an unusual spectacle: dressed in a priestly robe, he would stand in front of a set that looked like a mountain peak and give a stream-of-consciousness speech. *Slate* writers Andrew Kahn and Forrest Wickman compared this to the famous Sermon on the Mount, in which Jesus began to teach his disciples up on a mountainside. Some nights West would speak for 10 minutes and others for up to 25 minutes. Sometimes he would freestyle rap while at other times he performed more like a comedian at a club. Regardless of which kind of "sermon" he gave, West often ended with the message "If you believe you can do anything, put your hands up in the air right now."[3]

really is talented. . . . No one's near doing what he's doing, it's not even on the same planet."[4]

AN ELABORATE ROMANCE

From dropping albums to welcoming babies, 2013 was a big year in West's life. On October 21, 2013, just months after their daughter North was born, West proposed to Kim Kardashian. It was no ordinary proposal. West rented AT&T stadium in San Francisco, California, for the occasion. He had the message "PLEEASE MARRY MEEE!!!" on the Jumbotron. The Chicago Symphony played at the extravagant event.

If West's proposal was over-the-top, so was his multi-million-dollar wedding. The rehearsal dinner was held at the Palace of Versailles near Paris, France. On May 24, 2014, the wedding ceremony took place in Florence, Italy, at a sixteenth-century fortress called Forte di Belvedere. Among the many guests were rappers Common and Q-Tip, singer John Legend, and professional basketball player Carmelo Anthony. The power couple and baby North all wore clothes by Givenchy. Malika Haqq, a family friend, said of the event: "Kanye really went all out there with his love."[5]

McCartney, Rihanna, and West performed together at the 2015 Grammys.

West and Kardashian's love story has continued, and their family has grown. Their son, Saint, was born in Los Angeles on December 5, 2015. The family also expected a new addition in the fall of 2017.

WORKING WITH A BEATLE

During his musical career, West has collaborated with a variety of musicians. In 2014, he worked with former Beatle Paul McCartney on a song called "Only One." McCartney plays keyboard on the track. "Only One" is a tribute to West's young daughter, North, and is written from an unusual perspective— that of his deceased mother, Donda. West said about this song: "My mom was singing to me, and through me to my daughter." He also commented that his first name, *Kanye*, means "only one."[6] Kardashian says this is her favorite of all of her husband's songs.

The "Only One" music video starts with West running down a country road. It has a very sweet feel, a departure from many

FASHION TEACHER

West has inspired many in the fashion world throughout his career. In 2014, he had an opportunity to do some hands-on teaching at the Los Angeles Trade–Technical College. He taught fashion classes to meet a court-ordered sentence that included community service. He received this punishment after a fight he had with freelance photographer Daniel Ramos in 2013. West encouraged the students to use their youth to explore fashion, as well as critiquing celebrity designers who do not know how to sew or cut patterns. In one class, West led a three-hour discussion about fashion designers. In another, he shared his own experiences in the fashion industry.

of his other videos. West walks hand in hand with toddler North and sings rather than raps. Nature is also a focus throughout the video.

West collaborated with McCartney again in 2015 on a soulful yet catchy song titled "FourFiveSeconds." McCartney plays acoustic guitar, and Rihanna sings on the track, which some have described as "folk-pop-soul influenced."[7] Unlike nearly all of West's other songs, this one does not feature drums, giving it a gentler, more mellow feel.

HONORARY DOCTORATE

In May of 2015, Kanye West received an honorary doctorate from the School of the Art Institute of Chicago (SAIC). Dr. Lisa Wainwright, a professor who has served as dean of the faculty at SAIC, explained the choice to honor West by saying, "Here is this major figure in the cultural landscape promoting art school, this guy from Chicago saying art school is cool. . . . This man would have been a perfect SAIC student—he likes to shake people out of complacency."[8]

THE LIFE OF PABLO

Some artists might rest on their laurels after recording two songs with rock star royalty such as McCartney. But West was plugging away to create his next album, *The Life of Pablo*, which finally dropped on February 14, 2016. West compares himself in the album's title and in the track

West unveiled *The Life of Pablo* and a new season of his fashion line Yeezy together at a February 2016 event in New York City.

"No More Parties in L.A." to Pablo Picasso, a Spanish artist and creative genius.

West told fans that he would not be releasing *The Life of Pablo* as a CD but would make it available only by streaming. On February 14, the album was released exclusively on Tidal, a streaming service in which West is part owner. He also made it available on his website. One thing that was unusual about the album is that West continued to make changes to various tracks even after its initial release date. He tweeted on March 16, 2016: "Fixing Wolves 2day. . . . Worked on it for 3 weeks. Life Of Pablo is a living breathing changing creative expression."[9]

The Life of Pablo was led by the single "Famous." In an interview with *Vanity Fair*, West described the video for this song as a commentary on fame. But many found the ten-minute clip offensive. It shows likenesses of numerous celebrities nude and in bed together. The celebrities featured in the video range from West's wife, his friend Rihanna, and his ex-girlfriend Amber Rose to political figures such as George Bush and Donald Trump. Taylor Swift is also one of the people portrayed in the scene.

The Life of Pablo featured many guest artists, including the Weeknd, Chance the

Rapper, Rihanna, Chris Brown, and Frank Ocean. Critics raved about some tracks and disliked others. Many were amused by the song "I Love Kanye." Its lyrics reflect Kanye's complex personality and perhaps inner turmoil: "I hate the new Kanye, the bad mood Kanye/The always rude Kanye, spaz in the news Kanye/I miss the sweet Kanye, chop up the beats Kanye."[10] A *New York Times* review of the album talks about its "rambling, fearsome energy" and compares it to the website Tumblr, where many fragments are put together to make a finished project that is cohesive.[11] *Guardian* writer Nosheen Iqbal said: "Here's an album that is soulful, troubled, brilliant and, in plenty of ways, defines the tumultuous year we've had."[12]

Similar to all of West's earliest albums, *The Life of Pablo* sold well. The album debuted at the top of the *Billboard* 200 chart. British newspaper the *Guardian* named *The Life of Pablo* its Number 4 album of the year. In April 2017, it became West's eighth album to go platinum. Only time will tell if West was right when he said that

"The Famous video is one of the more disturbing 'artistic' efforts in recent memory. . . . It gives me such a sickening sense of dis-ease."[13]

–Actress Lena Dunham

West collaborator Frank Ocean is known for his experimental style, often featuring the electronic keyboard.

The Life of Pablo is more than the album of the year or even of the decade. "This is the album of the life," he said.[14]

THE KANYE EFFECT

West has been one of the most influential musicians of his generation. He has expanded people's visions of hip-hop since his earliest days as a producer and rapper. One of the ways he has done this is by introducing new instruments into hip-hop music, from French horns to cellos. As West learned more about orchestral music, he chose to share some of that knowledge with his fans, even when that may not have been the typical thing to do in the hip-hop genre.

Another way that West has expanded hip-hop music is through his lyrics. He made it more acceptable to discuss topics that had not been previously tackled in the genre. For example, before West's music, hip-hop artists did not really rap or sing about religion. The raging success of songs such as "Jesus Walks" made it clear, though, that it was not only acceptable to write lyrics about religion, but

West performed in his hometown of Chicago in 2016.

WIDE APPEAL

One of West's real talents is his ability to appeal to a broad audience. In 2009, West won a Teen Choice Award as the Choice Rap Artist. The award was decided by votes of young people ages 13 to 19. But it is not just teens or diehard rap fans who enjoy West's diverse mix of music. While still in the White House, President Barack Obama said, "Look, I love his music. He's incredibly creative."[2]

also fresh and cool to do so. Writer Neil Shah believes West "brought emotional honesty to rap."[1] From criticizing consumerism to talking about his own insecurities to speaking out against homophobia, West has not shied away from any topic.

Many executives in the music industry believed it was a deal breaker to have an artist like West not look the part of a typical rapper. Others questioned West's lyrics, which did not cover selling drugs, hustling, or street crime. However, West became a tremendous success, proving the naysayers wrong. He was confident that he had something unique to offer the musical world—and he was right. Despite his love-hate relationship with award ceremonies, West will go down in history as one of the most decorated musicians of an era. By 2017, West had been nominated for 68 Grammys and was the winner of 21 of them, tying him with Jay-Z as the top Grammy-winning rap artist of all time. Writer Scott Meslow commented on West's infamous behavior at various award ceremonies, including the Grammys, saying, "Thank the music gods we have Kanye West, agent of chaos, to inject some life into the proceedings."[3]

SERVING AS A MENTOR

> "I will go down as the voice of this generation, of this decade. I will be the loudest voice."[4]
>
> –Kanye West

West also has acted as a mentor and helped further the careers of a number of other musicians. He established his own music label, known as G.O.O.D. Music, in 2004. The acronym G.O.O.D. stands for Getting Out Our Dreams. The label's first official release was *Get Lifted*, John Legend's debut album. West signed artists who have become some of hip-hop's hottest acts, including Big Sean and Pusha T. Recent additions to the G.O.O.D. Music label include Tyga and Migos. West also signed Kacy Hill, a model and former dancer from his *Yeezus* tour.

At the 2015 Brit Awards, West praised the rappers from the United Kingdom. During his live performance, West performed with some British artists who are not well known in the United States, including Skepta and Novelist. British actor Idris Elba talked about the importance of

JEWELRY COLLECTION

West designs clothes for everyone from toddlers to well-heeled fashionistas around the globe. He also designs shoes for Adidas and Louis Vuitton. Beginning in 2017, West even launched his own jewelry collection, a collaboration with Jacob Arabo. West and Arabo's history goes way back. Arabo is mentioned in West's song "Touch the Sky." West said the inspiration for the jewelry collection came from the art of 1300s Florence, Italy, noting, "I wanted to create something that represented timeless love."[6]

the performance: "But with Kanye [bringing them onstage] it makes it easier. Everyone goes, 'OK, let's have a listen then.' It's wicked. I give Kanye mad props for doing that. I thought it was visionary of him."[5]

West also has encouraged the next generation of musicians through his charity work. In 2005, he established the Kanye West Foundation, aimed at reducing dropout rates in schools around the United States. The foundation's first initiative was a program called Loop Dreams. The program has several goals, including keeping musical instruments and instruction in the schools. In addition, the program aims to teach students who are considered at risk how to produce and write music while also helping them improve their academic skills. West also is a large donor to the nonprofit Donda's House, named after his mother.

The aim of Donda's House is to provide arts and literature instruction to youth. Within this nonprofit is a program called Got Bars, which works with aspiring artists on studio recording, creative writing, and wellness education.

FASHION MOGUL

West is a visionary in fashion as well. His unique style has been a part of his persona since his earliest days as a musician. When other rappers were wearing baggy pants and huge gold chains, West was sporting polo shirts and loafers. Whether wearing a leather skirt in concert or sporting his own brand of expensive sweatpants at an award ceremony, West puts himself out there on the fashion front. He is not afraid to experiment with his look, even when that brings on criticism.

West has been interested in learning more about the fashion industry, whether by attending many runway shows in Paris and New York or by interning at Fendi in Italy. In the fall of 2011, West's first collection was featured on the

> "Even for me as a successful musician, in order to make the transition [to working in fashion], it was really all but impossible. People always try to box you in to what they know you best for."[7]
>
> —Kanye West

West shared the stage with British performers during the 2015 Brit Awards.

runways of Paris. His designs at this show were described as "heavy" because of their zippers, beading, and leather and suede fabrics. But his first collection was well received within the fashion world. West was congratulated after

the show by Silvia and Delfina Delettrez Fendi, Italian
designers and family members affiliated with the Fendi
design house.

COLLECTING AWARDS

In addition to his 21 Grammys, West has also been nominated for and won many other awards throughout his musical career. Some of these awards come from the African-American community. For example, West has won five MOBO Awards (Music of Black Origin) as well as many BET (Black Entertainment Television) and Soul Train Awards. In the United States, West has earned American Music Awards and *Billboard* Music Awards, among many others. He also has received several international awards, such as three Brit Awards, an Echo Award from Germany, and a Meteor Ireland Music Award.

West continues to be nominated for many of his collaborations, such as "FourFiveSeconds" at the 2015 American Music Awards and "One Man Can Change the World" at the 2016 BET Awards. The latter was a collaboration with Big Sean and John Legend.

Since that first Paris runway show, West has continued to work on his own collections and fashion collaborations with other already-established labels. His Yeezy collections have made fashion news year after year. Just like his music, these collections vary from season to season. For example, in the Season 1 Collection of Yeezy, the military aspect of the clothes was essential. West's Fall 2015 fashion show featured models of many shapes and sizes on the runway. West continued to challenge catwalk conventionality with his Season 5 Yeezy collection. At New York Fashion Week in February 2017, his catwalk models included Halima Aden, a hijab-wearing

Muslim Somali American. But West does not just design fashion for adults. In 2017, he and his wife unveiled their Kids Supply line of hip toddler clothes. Given his passion for fashion, West is likely to continue designing his own collections for years to come.

WHAT'S NEXT?

In November 2016, West was hospitalized and treated for exhaustion in Los Angeles just hours after canceling the remainder of his Saint Pablo tour. The tour had been going since August. In the months that followed, West largely stayed out of the limelight. He also deleted his Twitter and Instagram social media accounts. Fellow musician and friend John Legend said, "I'm not gonna try to analyze what's happening with him. I just want him to

KANYE FOR PRESIDENT?

At the 2015 VMAs, Kanye West announced his plans to run for president in 2020. Since that time, many people have wondered whether he was serious. In November 2016, he repeated his intent to run. In previous interviews, West had said he did not have specific political views but instead had views on people and the truth. He stated, "I'm concerned about putting our concept of how to do the [president's] job in a new way and if no one will do it in that way, I will take position in 2020 and do it myself."[8]

In addition to his other creative pursuits, West has been and will continue to be a fixture in the fashion world for years.

do whatever he needs to do to feel better and to feel like he's ready to go again, because music needs him. The world needs him."[9]

Even though he kept a low profile for most of early 2017, West was reportedly working on his next album. In May 2017, several sources mentioned that he was finding inspiration for the album at a Wyoming mountaintop retreat. West teased people in 2016 with a title for the new album—*Turbo Grafx 16*—though that could certainly change. After all, change has been an essential part of West's excitement and charisma as a musician since he began. No doubt there is much that West has not done that he aims to accomplish. In his own words, "I haven't begun to scratch the surface of what I can create for the world."[10]

1977

On June 8, Kanye Omari West is born just outside of Atlanta, Georgia.

1987

Kanye spends a year in China.

1995

Kanye graduates from Polaris High School in Oak Lawn, Illinois.

2002

On October 23, West is seriously injured in a car accident in Los Angeles.

2004

On February 10, West's debut album, *The College Dropout*, is released.

2005

On February 13, West receives his first three Grammy Awards; on August 30, West's album *Late Registration* is released.

2006

On February 8, West wins three more Grammy Awards.

2007

On September 11, West releases his third studio album, *Graduation*; on November 10, West's mother, Donda, dies.

2008

In April, West kicks off his Glow in the Dark tour; on November 24, West releases his *808s & Heartbreak* album.

2009

On September 13, West interrupts Taylor Swift when she is accepting an award at the MTV Video Music Awards.

2010

On November 22, West releases his album *My Beautiful Dark Twisted Fantasy.*

2011

On August 8, West and Jay-Z release their joint album, *Watch the Throne.*

2013

On June 15, West's daughter, North, is born; on June 18, West's album *Yeezus* is released.

2014

On May 24, West marries Kim Kardashian in Italy.

2015

In May, West receives an honorary doctorate from the School of the Art Institute of Chicago; on August 30, Taylor Swift presents West with the MTV Video Vanguard Award; on December 5, West's son, Saint, is born.

2016

On February 14, West's album *The Life of Pablo* is released; in November, West cancels his Saint Pablo concert tour and is hospitalized and treated for exhaustion in Los Angeles.

2017

In April, *The Life of Pablo* becomes West's eighth album to go platinum; West expands his brand with a jewelry collection and a fashion line for toddlers; West continues to make new music.

FULL NAME

Kanye Omari West

DATE OF BIRTH

June 8, 1977

PLACE OF BIRTH

Douglasville, Georgia

PARENTS

Donda and Ray West

EDUCATION

- 1995 graduate of Polaris High School

- Briefly attended the American Academy of Art and Chicago State University but did not graduate.

MARRIAGE

Kim Kardashian (May 24, 2014)

CHILDREN

- North West

- Saint West

CAREER HIGHLIGHTS

Kanye West has had eight albums go platinum. He has won 21 Grammy Awards, as well as numerous other awards, including the 2015 MTV Video Vanguard Award.

ALBUMS

The College Dropout (2004), *Late Registration* (2005), *Graduation* (2007), *808s & Heartbreak* (2008), *My Beautiful Dark Twisted Fantasy* (2010), *Watch the Throne* (2011), *Yeezus* (2013), *The Life of Pablo* (2016)

CONTRIBUTION TO HIP-HOP

West has made many contributions to hip-hop, widening the variety of the instruments used and the topics covered in the lyrics within this genre's songs.

CONFLICTS

Over the years, West has had conflicts with paparazzi but is most known for his conflicts with fellow musician Taylor Swift.

QUOTE

"I will go down as the voice of this generation, of this decade. I will be the loudest voice."

—*Kanye West*

A&R

Artists and repertoire, a division of a record label responsible for finding new artists and signing them to the label.

AUTO-TUNE MACHINE

A machine that digitally corrects sounds.

DEBUT

The first album or publication by a musician or group.

HIP-HOP

A style of popular music that features rap with electronic backing.

HUSTLE

To get things, such as money, through illicit action, such as selling drugs.

MIXER

An audio machine used by DJs to balance the instruments and vocals of a song.

MIXTAPE

A compilation of unreleased tracks, freestyle rap music, and DJ mixes of songs.

MONTAGE

A sequence of film made up from several film selections.

PLATINUM

An album is certified platinum when it sells a million units.

PRODUCER

The person who supervises the sampling, mixing, and recording of music and also guides the performer.

PROTÉGÉ

A person who is supported and guided by a more experienced or influential person.

RAP

A type of music in which words are recited quickly and rhythmically, usually over an electronic, prerecorded backing.

STREAM-OF-CONSCIOUSNESS

A person's thoughts and conscious reactions to things, released as a continuous flow.

TURNTABLE

An electronic device consisting of a needle and a disk that spins. When the needle is placed on a vinyl record, it plays music.

SELECTED BIBLIOGRAPHY

Beaumont, Mark. *Kanye West: God & Monster*. London: Omnibus, 2015. Print.

Caramanica, Jon. "Behind Kanye's Mask." *New York Times*. New York Times, 11 June 2013. Web. 29 May 2017.

Cochrane, Lauren. "Kanye West's Fashion Journey." *Guardian*. Guardian, 12 Aug. 2011. Web. 14 May 2017.

Mukherjee, Roopali, and Sarah Banet-Weiser, eds. *Commodity Activism: Cultural Resistance in Neoliberal Times*. New York: NYU, 2012. Print.

West, Donda, and Karen Hunter. *Raising Kanye: Life Lessons from the Mother of a Hip-Hop Superstar*. New York: Pocket, 2007. Print.

FURTHER READINGS

Lynne, Douglas. *Kanye West: Grammy-Winning Hip-Hop Artist and Producer*. Minneapolis: Abdo, 2013. Print.

Schaller, Robert, Jr. *Kanye West: A Biography*. Westport, CT: Greenwood, 2008. Print.

ONLINE RESOURCES

Booklinks
NONFICTION NETWORK
FREE! ONLINE NONFICTION RESOURCES

To learn more about Kanye West, visit **abdobooklinks.com**. These links are routinely monitored and updated to provide the most current information available.

MORE INFORMATION

For more information on this subject, contact or visit the following organizations:

AMERICAN ACADEMY OF ART
332 S. Michigan Avenue
Chicago, IL 60604
312-461-0600
aaart.edu

Kanye West started his post–high school studies here. Visitors to the campus can do a tour and see works of art produced by students in a variety of media.

GRAMMY MUSEUM
800 W. Olympic Boulevard
Los Angeles, CA 90015
213-765-6800
grammymuseum.org

The Grammy Museum offers exhibits on the art and technology involved in recording music. Artists who have won Grammys, including Kanye West, are celebrated here.

NATIONAL MUSEUM OF HIP-HOP
244 Fifth Avenue, Suite 1255
New York, NY 10001
hiphopmuseum.org/contact

While this museum does not yet have a physical space to visit, it is active on social media and offers people the chance to look and learn more about hip-hop art, videos, and more.

SOURCE NOTES

CHAPTER 1. KANYE ALWAYS SURPRISES

1. Alex Heigl. "Kanye West to Receive Video Vanguard Award at MTV VMAs." *People*. People, 25 Aug. 2015. Web. 28 Aug. 2017.

2. Julia Brucculieri. "Kanye West to Receive Video Vanguard Award at 2015 MTV VMAs." *Huffpost*. HPMG News, 25 Aug. 2015. Web. 28 Aug. 2017.

3. "Power." *Genius*. Genius Media Group, n.d. Web. 28 Aug. 2017.

4. "Top 10 Outrageous Kanye West Moments." *Time*. Time, n.d. Web. 28 Aug. 2017.

5. "Video Vanguard Award 2015." *Streamable*. Streamable, n.d. Web. 28 Aug. 2017.

6. "Top 10 Outrageous Kanye West Moments." *Time*. Time, n.d. Web. 28 Aug. 2017.

7. Gil Kaufman. "Here's the Full Transcript of Kanye's Incredible VMA Vanguard Speech." *MTV News*. Viacom International, 31 Aug. 2015. Web. 28 Aug. 2017.

8. Ibid.

9. Suzannah Ramsdale. "'I Am God's Vessel': Kanye West's Most WTF Quotes." *Marie Claire*. Time, 18 Nov. 2016. Web. 31 Aug. 2017.

10. Gil Kaufman. "Here's the Full Transcript of Kanye's Incredible VMA Vanguard Speech." *MTV News*. Viacom International, 31 Aug. 2015. Web. 28 Aug. 2017.

CHAPTER 2. ATLANTA TO CHICAGO

1. Donda West and Karen Hunter. *Raising Kanye: Life Lessons from the Mother of a Hip-Hop Superstar*. New York: Pocket, 2007. Print. 71.

2. Mark Beaumont. *Kanye West: God & Monster*. London: Omnibus, 2015. Print. 26.

3. Donda West and Karen Hunter. *Raising Kanye: Life Lessons from the Mother of a Hip-Hop Superstar*. New York: Pocket, 2007. Print. 71.

4. Ibid. 63.

5. Kimberly Davis. "Kanye West: Hip-Hop's New Big Shot." *Ebony* Apr. 2005: 160. Print.

6. Mark Beaumont. *Kanye West: God & Monster*. London: Omnibus, 2015. Print. 20.

7. Donda West and Karen Hunter. *Raising Kanye: Life Lessons from the Mother of a Hip-Hop Superstar*. New York: Pocket, 2007. Print. 8.

CHAPTER 3. KEYBOARDS AND CONTACTS

1. Chris Martins. "Here's Kanye West Being Kanye West Before He Was Famous." *SPIN*. Billboard-Hollywood Reporter Media Group, 2 Nov. 2013. Web. 28 Aug. 2017.

2. Daniel D'Addario and Francesca Trianni. "Kanye West Talks Hope for Humanity's Future." *Time*. Time, 16 April 2015. Web. 28 Aug. 2017.

3. Nekesa Mumbi Moody. "The Arrogant Master of Hip-Hop." *VailDaily*. Swift Communications, 4 Aug. 2004. Web. 28 Aug. 2017.

4. Mark Beaumont. *Kanye West: God & Monster*. London: Omnibus, 2015. Print. 41–42.

5. Ibid. 36.

6. Ibid. 40.

7. Ibid. 39.

CHAPTER 4. SUCCESS, REJECTION, AND DROPPING OUT

1. Mark Beaumont. *Kanye West: God & Monster*. London: Omnibus, 2015. Print. 45.

2. Ibid.

3. Ibid. 46.

4. "Grav—Down to Earth CD." *CD Universe*. Muze, n.d. Web. 28 Aug. 2017.

5. Mark Beaumont. *Kanye West: God & Monster*. London: Omnibus, 2015. Print. 48.

6. Donda West and Karen Hunter. *Raising Kanye: Life Lessons from the Mother of a Hip-Hop Superstar*. New York: Pocket, 2007. Print. 118.

7. "Spaceship." *Genius*. Genius, n.d. Web. 28 Aug. 2017.

8. Mark Beaumont. *Kanye West: God & Monster*. London: Omnibus, 2015. Print. 51.

9. Donda West and Karen Hunter. *Raising Kanye: Life Lessons from the Mother of a Hip-Hop Superstar*. New York: Pocket, 2007. Print. 111–112.

CHAPTER 5. THE PRODUCER

1. Ian Halperin. *Kardashian Dynasty: The Controversial Rise of America's Royal Family*. New York: Simon and Schuster, 2016. Print. 203.

2. Lily Rothman. "Why Kanye West Had Trouble Getting a Record Deal." *Time*. Time, 10 Feb. 2016. Web. 28 Aug. 2017.

3. Ibid.

4. Donda West and Karen Hunter. *Raising Kanye: Life Lessons from the Mother of a Hip-Hop Superstar*. New York: Pocket, 2007. Print. 128.

5. Kanye West. "Never Let Me Down." *Google Play Music*. Google, n.d. Web. 28 Aug. 2017.

6. Mark Beaumont. *Kanye West: God & Monster*. London: Omnibus, 2015. Print. 95–96.

7. "Through the Wire." *Genius*. Genius Media Group, n.d. Web. 28 Aug. 2017.

8. Donda West and Karen Hunter. *Raising Kanye: Life Lessons from the Mother of a Hip-Hop Superstar*. New York: Pocket, 2007. Print. 122.

CHAPTER 6. HIGHLIGHTS AND LOW LIGHTS

1. Paul Cantor. "Kanye West's 'The College Dropout' at 10: Classic Track-by-Track Review." *Billboard*. Billboard, 10 Feb. 2014. Web. 28 Aug. 2017.

2. "On the Charts: Kanye's Worst Opening Sales Week Still Leads Yeezus to No. 1." *Radio.com*. CBS Radio, 26 June 2013. Web. 28 Aug. 2017.

3. Kelefa Sanneh. "CRITIC'S CHOICE/New CD's; No Reading and Writing, but Rapping Instead." *New York Times*. New York Times Company, 9 Feb. 2004. Web. 28 Aug. 2017.

4. Jeff Weiss. "A History of the Hip Hop Skit." *Red Bull Music Academy Daily*. Red Bull, 7 July 2015. Web. 28 Aug. 2017.

5. "TIME Cover: Hip-Hop's Class Act—Kanye West." *Time*. Time, 21 Aug. 2005. Web. 28 Aug. 2017.

6. "Kanye West Accepted Grammy for Best Rap Album." *YouTube*. YouTube, 12 Mar. 2011. Web. 28 Aug. 2017.

7. Ibid.

8. "Louis Vuitton Don." *Urban Dictionary*. Urban Dictionary, n.d. Web. 28 Aug. 2017.

9. Greg Kot. "Kanye West's New Album Audaciously Takes Hip-Hop into Uncharted Territory." *Chicago Tribune*. Chicago Tribune, 28 Aug. 2005. Web. 28 Aug. 2017.

10. Ibid.

11. Ibid.

12. Chris Harris. "Kanye West's Late Registration Tops Albums Chart—By a Mile." *MTV News*. Viacom International, 7 Sep. 2005. Web. 28 Aug. 2017.

13. Jon Caramanica. "The Education of Kanye West." *New York Times*. New York Times Company, 26 Aug. 2007. Web. 28 Aug. 2017.

14. Ernest Baker, et al. "The 25 Biggest First-Week Album Sales in Music History." *Complex*. Complex Media, 27 Mar. 2013. Web. 28 Aug. 2017.

15. "Kanye Crushes 50 Cent in Huge Album Sales Week." *Billboard*. Billboard-Hollywood Reporter Media Group, 18 Sep. 2007. Web. 28 Aug. 2017.

16. Madeline Boardman. "Kanye West Blames Himself for Mom Donda West's Death." *US Weekly*. American Media, 26 June 2015. Web. 28 Aug. 2017.

CHAPTER 7. HEALING AND LOVE

1. Mark Beaumont. *Kanye West: God & Monster*. London: Omnibus, 2015. Print. 255.

2. MTV News Staff. "Kanye West's Ex-Fiancee Alexis Phifer Talks about Breakup." *MTV News*. Viacom International, 21 Apr. 2008. Web. 28 Aug. 2017.

3. Jeff Weiss. "First Thoughts on Kanye West's 808s & Heartbreak." *LA Weekly*. LA Weekly, 16 Oct. 2008. Web. 28 Aug. 2017.

4. Elias Leight. "8 Ways the 808 Drum Machine Changed Pop Music." *Rolling Stone*. Rolling Stone, 6 Dec. 2016. Web. 28 Aug. 2017.

5. "Pink." *Twitter*. Twitter, 13 Sep. 2009. Web. 28 Aug. 2017.

6. Jeff Weiss. "First Thoughts on Kanye West's 808s & Heartbreak." *LA Weekly*. LA Weekly, 16 Oct. 2008. Web. 28 Aug. 2017.

7. Jake Woolf. "5 Years Later, Is *My Beautiful Dark Twisted Fantasy* Really Kanye West's Best Album?" *GQ*. Condé Nast, 22 Nov. 2015. Web. 28 Aug. 2017.

8. Lauren Cochrane. "Kanye West's Fashion Journey." *Guardian*. Guardian News and Media Limited, 12 Aug. 2011. Web. 28 Aug. 2017.

9. Jake Woolf. "5 Years Later, Is *My Beautiful Dark Twisted Fantasy* Really Kanye West's Best Album?" *GQ*. Condé Nast, 22 Nov. 2015. Web. 28 Aug. 2017.

10. Jon Caramanica. "Two Titans Share the Seat of Power." *New York Times*. New York Times Company, 9 Aug. 2011. Web. 28 Aug. 2017.

11. Mark Beaumont. *Kanye West: God & Monster*. London: Omnibus, 2015. Print. 351–352.

12. Libby Hill. "Kimye: a Love Story Timeline." *Rolling Stone*. Rolling Stone, 8 July 2015. Web. 28 Aug. 2017.

CHAPTER 8. BEATLES AND BABIES

1. Suzannah Ramsdale. "'I Am God's Vessel': Kanye West's Most WTF Quotes." *Marie Claire*. Time, 18 Nov. 2016. Web. 31 Aug. 2017.

2. Jon Pareles. "A Fighter Returns with Angrier Air Punches." *New York Times*. New York Times Company, 16 June 2013. Web. 28 Aug. 2017.

3. Andrew Kahn and Forrest Wickman. "The Gospel According to Yeezus." *Slate*. Slate Group, n.d. Web. 28 Aug. 2017.

4. Lou Reed. "Lou Reed on Kanye West's Yeezus: 'It Brings Tears to My Eyes.'" *Guardian*. Guardian News and Media Limited, 3 July 2013. Web. 28 Aug. 2017.

5. "Kim Kardashian and Kanye West Wedding Costs: PEOPLE Breaks Down the Bill." *People*. Time, 25 May 2014. Web. 28 Aug. 2017.

6. Jason Newman. "Hear Paul McCartney and Kanye West's Emotional Ballad 'Only One.'" *Rolling Stone*. Rolling Stone, 1 Jan. 2015. Web. 28 Aug. 2017.

7. "Kanye West." *Biography*. Biography, n.d. Web. 28 Aug. 2017.

8. Christopher Borrelli. "School of Art Institute to Award Kanye West Honorary Doctorate." *Chicago Tribune*. Chicago Tribune, 17 Mar. 2015. Web. 28 Aug. 2017.

9. Charlotte Wilder. "The Ongoing, Messy Release of Kanye West's 'The Life of Pablo,' Explained." *USA Today*. USA Today, 1 Apr. 2016. Web. 28 Aug. 2017.

10. Nosheen Iqbal. "Best Albums of 2016: No. 4 The Life of Pablo by Kanye West." *Guardian*. Guardian News and Media Limited, 13 Dec. 2016. Web. 28 Aug. 2017.

11. Jon Caramanica. "Review: Kanye West's 'The Life of Pablo,' Songs of Praise and Self." *New York Times*. New York Times Company, 14 Feb. 2016. Web. 28 Aug. 2017.

12. Nosheen Iqbal. "Best Albums of 2016: No. 4 The Life of Pablo by Kanye West." *Guardian*. Guardian News and Media Limited, 13 Dec. 2016. Web. 28 Aug. 2017.

13. Maria Cavassuto. "Lena Dunham Slams Kanye West's 'Disturbing' 'Famous' Music Video." *Variety*. Penske Business Media, 27 June 2016. Web. 28 Aug. 2017.

14. Samantha Grossman. "Now You Can Have Your Very Own Custom Kanye Album Cover." *Time*. Time, 12 Feb. 2016. Web. 28 Aug. 2017.

CHAPTER 9. THE KANYE EFFECT

1. Neil Shah. "The Case for Kanye." *Wall Street Journal*. Dow Jones & Company, 9 Feb. 2016. Web. 28 Aug. 2017.

2. Esther Lee. "President Obama Calls Out Kanye West: 'I Don't Think I've Got His Home Number.'" *US Weekly*. American Media, 13 Mar. 2015. Web. 28 Aug. 2017.

3. Scott Meslow. "Kanye West, Hero of the Grammys." *Week*. Week, 9 Feb. 2015. Web. 28 Aug. 2017.

4. Suzannah Ramsdale. "'I Am God's Vessel': Kanye West's Most WTF Quotes." *Marie Claire*. Time, 18 Nov. 2016. Web. 31 Aug. 2017.

5. "Idris Elba Calls Kanye West's 2015 Brit Awards Performance a 'Visionary Salute' to Grime." *MOBO*. MOBO, n.d. Web. 28 Aug. 2017.

6. Trace William Cowen. "Kanye West Launches First Yeezy Jewelry Collection." *Complex*. Complex Media, 7 Apr. 2017. Web. 28 Aug. 2017.

7. "The Best Commencement Speeches, Ever." *NPR*. NPR, n.d. Web. 28 Aug. 2017.

8. McKenna Aiello. "Kanye West Still Has Plans to Run for President in 2020." *E! News*. E! Entertainment Television, 18 Nov. 2016. Web. 28 Aug. 2017.

9. Deepa Lakshmin. "John Legend Opens Up About Kanye West: 'Music Needs Him.'" *MTV News*. Viacom International, 30 Dec. 2016. Web. 28 Aug. 2017.

10. "'Top of the Pyramid?' Kanye West Speaks Exclusively in the New Issue of Q." *Q*. Bauer Consumer Media, 25 June 2015. Web. 28 Aug. 2017.

ABOUT THE AUTHOR

From ESP to vampires, Alicia Klepeis loves to research fun and out-of-the-ordinary topics that make nonfiction exciting for readers. Alicia began her career at the National Geographic Society. She is the author of more than 60 children's books, including *Bizarre Things We've Called Medicine, Goblins, Understanding Saudi Arabia Today*, and *The World's Strangest Foods*. Her middle-grade historical novel, *A Time for Change*, was released in 2016. She has also written more than 100 articles in magazines, such as *National Geographic Kids*. Alicia is currently working on several projects involving unusual animals, American history, and circus science. She lives with her family in upstate New York.